Ignite the Flame

Ignite the Flame

Maddison Mayberry

Contents

1

The Foundation of Communication

Understanding the Importance of Communication

In any intimate relationship, communication serves as the bedrock upon which all forms of connection are built. For couples seeking to ignite their sexual passion, understanding the nuances of communication is essential. Effective communication allows partners to express their desires, preferences, and boundaries, creating a safe space for exploration and vulnerability. It enables couples to discuss their fantasies openly, fostering an environment where both partners feel valued and heard. This understanding not only enhances their emotional bond but also deepens their physical connection, leading to more fulfilling sexual experiences.

Initiating conversations about sex can be daunting, but it is a crucial step toward maintaining incredible intimacy. Couples should approach these discussions with curiosity rather than judgment, asking open-ended questions that encourage dialogue. For instance, sharing what feels pleasurable or discussing fantasies can lead to exciting discoveries about each other's desires. By practicing active listening and responding with empathy, partners can create a dynamic where both feel comfortable sharing their needs, leading to a more adventurous and satisfying sex life.

Moreover, communication techniques can significantly enhance emotional connection, which is vital for sexual satisfaction. When couples engage in meaningful conversations about their feelings and experiences, they cultivate a deeper understanding of one another. This emotional intimacy lays the groundwork for exploring physical intimacy. Using "I" statements, expressing vulnerabilities, and validating each other's feelings can transform how partners relate to each other, making their sexual encounters not just physical but emotionally fulfilling as well.

Incorporating elements such as anticipation and foreplay into sexual communication is another vital aspect. Building anticipation can heighten desire and excitement, making the eventual encounter more thrilling. Couples can communicate their plans for a romantic evening or unexpected surprises, using teasing language or suggestive texts to enhance excitement. This playful exchange not only boosts arousal but also reinforces the connection between partners, encouraging them to look forward to their intimate moments together.

Lastly, communicating about the use of toys and accessories can open up new avenues for pleasure. Discussing preferences or boundaries related to these items can lead to enhanced sexual experiences and a greater sense of adventure in the bedroom. It's essential for couples to be open about their willingness to explore and to ensure that both partners feel comfortable with the choices made.

This openness fosters a collaborative spirit, where both individuals contribute to creating a more satisfying and exciting sexual life, ultimately reinforcing their bond and commitment to one another.

Barriers to Effective Communication

Effective communication is the cornerstone of a fulfilling sexual relationship, yet numerous barriers can impede this vital exchange between partners. These barriers often stem from misunderstandings, preconceived notions, and emotional baggage that couples may carry into their intimate interactions. Recognizing these challenges is the first step towards fostering an environment where open dialogue can flourish, ultimately enhancing both intimacy and sexual satisfaction. By addressing these barriers constructively, couples can pave the way for deeper connection and more fulfilling experiences.

One significant barrier to effective communication is the fear of vulnerability. Many individuals hesitate to express their desires and fantasies due to concerns about judgment or rejection. This fear can create a cycle of silence, where unspoken needs lead to frustration and resentment. Couples can overcome this barrier by creating a safe space for dialogue, where both partners feel respected and valued. Practicing active listening without interruption and affirming each other's feelings can help build trust, allowing for more honest discussions about sexual preferences and boundaries.

Another common obstacle is the influence of societal norms and expectations surrounding sex. Couples may find themselves adhering to outdated beliefs about what constitutes a "normal" sexual relationship, which can stifle creativity and exploration. To navigate this, partners should engage in open conversations about their individual beliefs and desires, recognizing that every relationship is unique. Embracing a mindset of curiosity and exploration encourages partners to share their fantasies and discuss the incorporation of toys or role play, ultimately enriching their sexual experiences.

Emotional disconnect can also pose a significant barrier to effective communication in intimate settings. When partners are preoccupied with unresolved conflicts or emotional issues, they may struggle to engage fully during intimate moments.

It is essential for couples to prioritize emotional check-ins, ensuring that both partners feel heard and understood outside of the bedroom. By regularly addressing emotional needs, couples can cultivate a deeper emotional connection that directly impacts their sexual satisfaction, leading to more fulfilling and passionate encounters.

Lastly, the challenge of maintaining excitement and anticipation in long-term relationships can hinder open communication about sexual needs. As routines become established, partners may fall into predictable patterns that diminish excitement. To counteract this, couples should actively discuss ways to incorporate spontaneity into their intimate lives. This might involve brainstorming new experiences, exploring fantasies together, or setting aside time for mindful practices that enhance sexual awareness. By openly sharing their thoughts on maintaining excitement and addressing any feelings of stagnation, partners can reignite their passion and strengthen their bond, leading to incredible sexual experiences together.

Creating a Safe Space for Dialogue

Creating a safe space for dialogue is essential for couples seeking to enhance their intimacy and sexual satisfaction. This sanctuary allows both partners to express their desires, fears, and fantasies without judgment. Establishing this environment begins with mutual respect and understanding, ensuring that both individuals feel valued and heard. When couples prioritize open communication, they lay the groundwork for deeper emotional connections, which are vital for maintaining sexual excitement and exploring new dimensions of their relationship.

To initiate this safe space, couples should agree on some ground rules for discussions about intimacy. These guidelines can include listening without interrupting, refraining from criticism, and using "I" statements to express feelings rather than placing blame. For example, instead of saying "You never want to try anything new," one might say, "I feel excited about exploring new experiences together." Such language fosters a more constructive conversation, allowing both partners to share their thoughts and feelings openly. By reinforcing these rules, couples can create an atmosphere of trust that encourages vulnerability.

Maintaining this safe space requires ongoing effort and commitment from both partners. Regular check-ins can help ensure that communication remains open and effective. Couples might set aside dedicated time each week to discuss their relationship and intimacy, focusing on what feels good and what could be improved. This practice not only strengthens emotional bonds but also helps partners stay attuned to each other's needs and desires. Over time, these conversations can lead to a greater understanding of each other's fantasies and preferences, enriching the sexual experience.

As couples delve into dialogue about their sexual relationship, they may find it helpful to explore topics such as the role of emotional connection in sexual satisfaction. Discussing how feelings of love, trust, and safety contribute to a fulfilling sexual experience can deepen intimacy. Couples can also share their thoughts on how to incorporate toys and accessories into their experiences, enhancing pleasure and excitement. By fostering a culture of curiosity and exploration, partners can discover new ways to bring joy into their sexual lives.

Ultimately, creating a safe space for dialogue transforms not only the couple's communication but also their overall relationship. This environment encourages partners to maintain sexual excitement in long-term relationships by allowing them to share fantasies, explore new techniques, and embrace mindfulness practices that enhance their experiences together. By prioritizing open dialogue, couples can ignite the flame of passion, ensuring that their connection remains strong and vibrant throughout the years.

2

Initiating Incredible Sex

Reading the Signals

Reading the signals between partners is essential for cultivating intimacy and enhancing sexual experiences. Couples often miss the subtle cues that indicate desire, comfort, and enthusiasm. Learning to interpret these signals can transform a relationship, creating an environment where both partners feel valued and understood. Observing body language, vocal tones, and even emotional expressions can provide insight into what each partner wants or needs. By honing the ability to read these signals, couples can initiate and maintain incredible sexual connections that are responsive and fulfilling.

Understanding the non-verbal cues in a relationship is crucial. These cues often communicate feelings far more effectively than words. For instance, leaning in closer, maintaining eye contact, or even playful touches can indicate attraction and readiness for intimacy. It is essential for partners to cultivate awareness of these signals, as they can lead to deeper emotional connections. When partners feel safe and attuned to one another, they are more likely to express their desires and boundaries openly, which enhances the overall experience of intimacy.

Effective communication techniques play a pivotal role in interpreting these signals accurately. Couples can benefit from establishing a safe space for open dialogue about their sexual desires, needs, and limits. This might involve asking questions and seeking clarification, which not only helps in understanding each other's signals but also strengthens the emotional bond. Regular check-ins about preferences and fantasies can encourage partners to share their thoughts and feelings without fear of judgment, leading to a more satisfying sexual experience.

Incorporating fantasy and role play can also be a powerful way to read and respond to each other's signals. Engaging in these activities requires a high level of trust and communication, as partners explore new dimensions of their sexual relationship. By discussing fantasies openly, couples can gauge each other's comfort levels and desires. This openness fosters a playful atmosphere where partners are more likely to express their wants and needs, making it easier to read and respond to signals that arise during these explorations.

Ultimately, maintaining sexual excitement and connection in long-term relationships hinges on the ability to read and respond to each other's signals continuously. Mindfulness practices can enhance this process by encouraging partners to be present and attuned to each other's emotional and physical states. By creating an environment where both partners feel heard and understood, couples can build anticipation and excitement, making their sexual experiences not only incredible but also deeply fulfilling. This ongoing practice of reading signals and responding with care can strengthen the foundation of their relationship, leading to lasting intimacy and satisfaction.

Approaching the Topic with Confidence

Approaching the topic of intimacy and sexual desires can often feel daunting for couples. However, tackling this subject with confidence is essential for fostering a deeper emotional and physical connection. Begin by recognizing that open communication is a cornerstone of any healthy relationship. By setting the stage for an honest dialogue, you create an environment where both partners feel safe to express their thoughts and desires. This proactive approach not only diminishes anxiety but also encourages vulnerability, which can lead to a richer, more fulfilling sexual experience.

To initiate these conversations, it's important to choose the right moment. Avoid bringing up sensitive topics during stressful times or when distractions abound. Instead, create a relaxed atmosphere where both partners can engage without interruptions. This might mean planning a special date night or finding quiet time at home. Being intentional about when and how you discuss intimacy allows both partners to be present and fully engaged in the conversation, fostering a sense of connection that enhances emotional intimacy.

Confidence in communication also stems from understanding your own desires and boundaries. Before broaching the subject, take time to reflect on what you want from your intimate life. This self-awareness enables you to articulate your thoughts clearly and confidently. When both partners approach the conversation with a solid understanding of their needs, it sets the stage for a more productive dialogue. It also shows respect for one another's feelings, making it easier to explore fantasies or introduce new elements into your sexual experiences, such as toys or role play.

As the conversation unfolds, it's vital to practice active listening. This means not only hearing what your partner says but also validating their feelings and encouraging them to share more. Acknowledging your partner's thoughts fosters trust and reinforces the idea that both partners' needs are important. This back-and-forth exchange can bring clarity to both partners, allowing for a deeper exploration of what enhances sexual satisfaction and builds anticipation. By emphasizing emotional connection during these discussions, couples can create a solid foundation for incredible sex.

Finally, maintaining this confidence over time requires ongoing commitment to communication. Regular check-ins about intimacy can help partners stay attuned to each other's evolving needs and desires. This practice not only nurtures emotional bonds but also keeps the sexual spark alive, even in long-term relationships. By continually engaging in open dialogue, couples can explore new fantasies, experiment with different techniques, and incorporate elements that enhance pleasure, ensuring that their intimate life remains vibrant and fulfilling.

Setting the Mood for Desire

Setting the mood for desire is a crucial step in enhancing intimacy and igniting passion within a relationship. Couples often overlook the importance of creating an environment that fosters connection and sensuality. To initiate incredible sex, it is essential to establish a space that encourages openness and vulnerability. This might involve dimming the lights, playing soft music, or ensuring privacy from distractions. By intentionally cultivating a romantic atmosphere, partners can elevate their emotional connection and enhance their sexual experiences.

Communication plays a pivotal role in setting the mood for desire. Engaging in open conversations about each partner's needs and fantasies can create a deeper emotional bond. Sharing thoughts about what excites both individuals allows for a more tailored experience. Couples should feel empowered to express their desires and boundaries, ensuring that both partners are on the same page. This dialogue not only strengthens intimacy but also builds trust, which is foundational for a fulfilling sexual relationship.

Exploring fantasy and role play can also be a powerful tool in setting the mood for desire. Couples can discuss their fantasies in a safe space, allowing them to explore new dimensions of their relationship. This creative exploration can lead to heightened arousal and anticipation, as partners step outside their usual routines. Whether it's dressing up, assuming different roles, or simply trying something new, these activities can enhance the excitement surrounding intimacy and invigorate the sexual dynamic.

Building anticipation is an art in itself, and foreplay is where this truly begins. Taking the time to engage in acts of affection, such as kissing, touching, or whispering sweet nothings can set the tone for a passionate encounter. The act of slowly unveiling desire through foreplay not only heightens physical sensations but also deepens emotional connections. Couples should embrace the journey of intimacy rather than rushing to the destination, as this can transform the overall experience into something truly memorable.

Incorporating toys and accessories can further enhance pleasure and excitement within the bedroom. Couples might consider introducing elements that stimulate the senses, such as scented candles, silk sheets, or sensual oils. These additions can create a more immersive experience, allowing partners to explore their desires together. By maintaining an open mindset towards new experiences and incorporating mindfulness practices, couples can cultivate an enriched sexual atmosphere that keeps desire alive. This continuous effort to enhance intimacy ensures that the flame of passion burns brightly, even in long-term relationships.

3

Techniques for Enhanced Intimacy

Active Listening Skills

Active listening is a vital skill for couples seeking to deepen their intimacy and enhance their sexual experiences. It goes beyond merely hearing words; it involves fully engaging with your partner to understand their feelings and desires. By practicing active listening, couples can create a safe space where both partners feel valued and understood, fostering an environment conducive to open communication about sexual needs and fantasies. This practice lays the foundation for a robust emotional connection, which is essential for achieving satisfaction in the bedroom.

To cultivate active listening skills, partners should prioritize being present during conversations. This means minimizing distractions, whether they are physical, like smartphones, or mental, like worries about the day ahead. When couples dedicate time to truly listen to one another, they communicate their willingness to invest in the relationship. Techniques such as maintaining eye contact, nodding, and using affirming gestures can signal to your partner that you are not only hearing but are also engaged in what they are saying. This engagement can lead to deeper conversations about desires and boundaries, necessary components for exploring fantasies and role play in a relationship.

Another crucial aspect of active listening is the practice of reflecting back what your partner has said. This can take the form of paraphrasing their words or summarizing their feelings. For example, if your partner shares a concern about sexual excitement waning in your relationship, responding with, "It sounds like you're feeling a bit disconnected and are looking for ways to reignite that spark," shows that you are not only listening but are also striving to understand their emotional state. This technique reinforces the emotional bond and encourages further dialogue, ultimately leading to a more satisfying sexual relationship.

Moreover, active listening involves asking open-ended questions that invite your partner to elaborate on their thoughts and feelings. Instead of yes-or-no questions, encourage deeper discussions by asking, "What are some things you've always wanted to try together?" or "How do you feel when we engage in foreplay?" These kinds of questions not only promote intimacy but also help couples explore new dimensions of their sexual relationship, such as incorporating toys and accessories for enhanced pleasure. Through this exploration, partners can better understand each other's preferences and fantasies, creating opportunities for shared experiences that deepen their connection.

In summary, active listening is a powerful tool for couples aiming to enhance their sexual relationship. By being present, reflecting back feelings, and asking open-ended questions, partners can foster a deeper emotional connection that enhances not only communication but also sexual satisfaction. As couples develop these skills, they will likely find that their sexual experiences become richer and more fulfilling, allowing them to maintain excitement in their long-term relationship. Embracing active listening not only strengthens the bond between partners but also sets the stage for incredible sex that is deeply rooted in mutual understanding and respect.

Verbal and Non-Verbal Cues

In the realm of intimacy, the nuances of communication extend beyond mere words. Verbal and non-verbal cues play a critical role in how couples connect and express their desires. Understanding these cues can ignite passion and deepen emotional bonds, transforming ordinary moments into extraordinary experiences. Couples can enhance their sexual relationship by becoming more attuned to each other's signals, creating a safe space for exploring fantasies and desires.

Verbal communication is a powerful tool for initiating and maintaining incredible sex. The way partners talk to each other can set the tone for their intimate encounters. Openly discussing preferences, boundaries, and desires fosters a climate of trust. Couples should practice using clear and affirmative language when expressing what feels good, what excites them, and what they wish to explore together. Encouraging each other to speak freely about fantasies or new ideas not only enhances sexual satisfaction but also strengthens emotional connections, making each partner feel valued and understood.

Non-verbal cues, on the other hand, are equally significant in conveying desire and affection. Body language, eye contact, and even the simple act of touch can communicate feelings that words may not adequately express. A gentle caress or a lingering gaze can speak volumes about attraction and encouragement. Couples should pay attention to these subtleties, observing how their partner reacts to different forms of touch or intimacy. By attuning themselves to each other's non-verbal signals, partners can build anticipation and create an environment ripe for exploring new dimensions of pleasure.

Moreover, the combination of verbal and non-verbal cues can enhance the experience of foreplay and intimacy. As couples engage in playful banter or whispered secrets, they can amplify the excitement leading up to sexual encounters. This interplay not only builds anticipation but also fosters a deeper emotional connection, allowing partners to feel more in sync. Incorporating flirty gestures, playful touches, and teasing remarks during these moments can heighten arousal and create a shared sense of adventure, making every encounter more thrilling.

Ultimately, mastering the art of communication through both verbal and non-verbal cues empowers couples to maintain sexual excitement in long-term relationships. By continuously engaging with each other, expressing desires openly, and responding to each other's signals, partners can cultivate a vibrant and satisfying sexual connection. This ongoing dialogue is essential for sustaining intimacy, ensuring that the flame of passion remains alive, and allowing both partners to explore their fantasies and desires fully.

Expressing Needs and Desires

Expressing needs and desires is a vital aspect of fostering intimacy and enhancing sexual satisfaction in a relationship. Couples often find themselves navigating the complexities of communication, especially when it comes to discussing their sexual preferences and fantasies. The first step in this process is to create a safe and open environment where both partners feel comfortable sharing their thoughts. This involves active listening, where each person is encouraged to express their needs without fear of judgment or rejection. By establishing this supportive atmosphere, couples can lay the groundwork for deeper emotional connections that are essential for incredible sex.

One effective technique for expressing desires is the use of "I" statements. Instead of saying "You never do this," reframe it to "I feel closer to you when we explore this together." This approach not only reduces defensiveness but also emphasizes the emotional impact of their actions on one another.

By focusing on personal feelings and experiences, couples can engage in more meaningful conversations about their sexual preferences. Additionally, discussing desires outside of the bedroom can help normalize these conversations, making it easier to transition to more intimate discussions when the moment arises.

Exploring fantasies and role play can be an exciting way to express needs and desires. Couples should approach this topic with curiosity and openness, understanding that fantasies are often an expression of deeper longings. Sharing fantasies can deepen emotional bonds and increase sexual excitement, as partners learn more about each other's inner worlds. It is crucial to discuss boundaries and consent before diving into role play, ensuring that both partners feel comfortable and respected. This exploration not only enhances sexual experiences but also promotes a sense of adventure and playfulness within the relationship.

Another key element in expressing needs and desires is the art of anticipation. Building excitement through foreplay can transform the sexual experience and heighten intimacy. Couples can communicate their preferences for foreplay techniques, discussing what makes them feel desired and excited. This can include everything from specific touches to verbal affirmations. By focusing on the buildup, couples can create a more fulfilling sexual experience that satisfies both partners' needs. Engaging in playful banter and teasing can also serve to enhance anticipation, making the eventual intimacy even more rewarding.

Lastly, incorporating mindfulness practices can greatly enhance the way couples express their needs and desires. Being present in the moment allows partners to fully experience their sensations and emotions during intimate moments. Mindfulness can help individuals articulate their needs more clearly, as they become more in tune with their bodies and feelings. Practices such as deep breathing, meditation, or even guided intimacy exercises can foster a deeper connection and enhance sexual experiences. By prioritizing these practices, couples can cultivate an environment where expressing needs and desires becomes a natural and fulfilling part of their sexual relationship.

4

Exploring Fantasy and Role Play

Understanding Each Other's Desires

Understanding each other's desires is a fundamental aspect of cultivating intimacy and enhancing sexual satisfaction in a relationship. Couples often find themselves navigating the complex landscape of individual preferences, fantasies, and needs. To truly connect with one another, it is essential to engage in open and honest communication about what each partner desires, both emotionally and sexually. This dialogue not only fosters a deeper understanding but also creates a safe space for vulnerability, allowing partners to express their needs without fear of judgment.

One effective way to initiate conversations about desires is through active listening. Couples should create an environment where both partners feel comfortable sharing their thoughts and feelings. This involves not just hearing the words spoken but truly understanding the emotions and intentions behind them. By practicing active listening, partners can validate each other's experiences and create a stronger emotional connection. This connection is crucial, as it lays the groundwork for exploring sexual desires that may be rooted in deeper emotional needs, thus enhancing overall satisfaction.

In addition to verbal communication, exploring fantasies and role play can significantly enrich a couple's sexual experiences. Each partner may have unique fantasies that they have hesitated to share for fear of judgment. However, discussing these desires can lead to exciting opportunities for exploration and experimentation. Couples should approach these discussions with an open mind, viewing them as a chance to enhance their intimacy rather than a potential source of conflict. By embracing each other's fantasies, couples can build anticipation, deepen their emotional bond, and invigorate their sexual encounters.

Building anticipation is also an essential element of understanding each other's desires. Foreplay, both emotional and physical, plays a critical role in this process. Engaging in activities that excite and stimulate both partners can create a heightened sense of desire, transforming routine intimacy into something extraordinary. Couples should explore various forms of foreplay, including playful teasing, sensual massages, or even intimate conversations that stimulate the mind. Incorporating these practices encourages partners to tune into each other's responses, fostering a shared experience that strengthens their connection and enhances pleasure.

Finally, it is important for couples to continually check in with each other about their evolving desires and preferences. As relationships grow and change, so too do individual needs and fantasies. Regularly revisiting these conversations ensures that both partners feel heard and valued, contributing to a lasting sense of intimacy. By prioritizing open communication and actively engaging with each other's desires, couples can ignite the flame of passion in their relationship, leading to a fulfilling and satisfying sexual experience that endures over time.

Setting Boundaries and Safe Words

Setting boundaries in a sexual relationship is essential for creating a safe and enjoyable environment for both partners. Establishing clear limits allows couples to explore their desires without fear of crossing emotional or physical lines. Open discussions about preferences, fantasies, and limits can foster a deeper understanding of each other's needs. Couples should set aside time to talk about their boundaries, ensuring that both partners feel heard and respected. This foundational step not only strengthens intimacy but also enhances sexual satisfaction by providing a framework within which both individuals can thrive.

Safe words serve as an important tool in establishing boundaries, especially in the context of exploring fantasies or engaging in role play. A safe word is a pre-agreed term that either partner can use to signal the need to pause or stop an activity. Choosing a word that is easy to remember and unlikely to come up in regular conversation is crucial. Common choices include "red," "yellow," or something playful that suits the couple's dynamic. The key is that both partners feel comfortable using the safe word without fear of judgment or disappointment. This practice builds trust and allows for a deeper dive into exploration while ensuring both partners can maintain control over the experience.

Incorporating safe words into your sexual relationship is not just about the physical aspects; it also enhances emotional connection. When both partners know they can voice their discomfort at any point, it creates an environment of trust and vulnerability. This emotional safety can encourage partners to express their fantasies more freely, leading to a more fulfilling sexual experience. Additionally, discussing and revisiting boundaries regularly can help couples adjust to changing comfort levels, ensuring that both partners feel secure as they experiment with new activities or fantasies.

Communication about boundaries and safe words can also enhance the anticipation and excitement that comes with foreplay. When couples openly express their desires and limits, they can create a more dynamic and engaging sexual experience. Knowing what to expect can heighten arousal and create a sense of adventure. Couples might even incorporate the concept of safe words into their foreplay routine, using them playfully to tease and build anticipation. This not only reinforces the importance of boundaries but also adds an element of fun and excitement to the relationship.

Ultimately, understanding the importance of setting boundaries and using safe words is a vital aspect of maintaining sexual excitement in long-term relationships. As partners grow together, their desires and limits may evolve. Regularly revisiting these discussions ensures that both partners remain in sync, allowing for continued exploration and satisfaction. By prioritizing open communication, couples can turn what might seem like a daunting task into an opportunity for connection, enhancing their emotional bond while navigating the complexities of their sexual relationship.

Creative Scenarios to Try

Creative scenarios can serve as powerful tools for couples looking to reignite their sexual connection and deepen their intimacy. Engaging in imaginative role play or fantasy can break the routine and infuse your relationship with excitement. Begin by discussing fantasies or scenarios that intrigue both partners, creating a safe space where each person's desires can be expressed without judgment. This open dialogue fosters emotional connection and ensures that both partners feel heard and valued, setting the stage for a more fulfilling sexual experience.

One effective scenario to explore is the classic "stranger" role play, where partners can take on new identities. By pretending to meet for the first time, couples can strip away the familiarity of their everyday lives and embrace the thrill of discovery. This playful approach allows for a fresh perspective on attraction and can reignite initial sparks. Prepare for this scenario by choosing distinctive outfits, crafting backstories, and even selecting a venue that enhances the experience. This not only builds anticipation but also serves as a reminder of the excitement that brought you together in the first place.

Another scenario involves creating a romantic treasure hunt that leads to intimate encounters. By leaving clues around the house or a chosen location, couples can enjoy a sense of adventure and playfulness. Each clue can lead to a small gift or a sensual note, culminating in a final surprise that brings the couple together for an intimate moment. This activity encourages teamwork and creativity, allowing partners to express their desires and fantasies in an engaging way. The element of surprise heightens arousal and reinforces emotional bonds, contributing to a more satisfying sexual experience.

Incorporating mindfulness practices into your sexual relationship can also enhance creativity in the bedroom. Consider setting aside time to connect through meditation or breathing exercises before engaging in intimate activities. This practice encourages partners to focus on their sensations and the emotional connection they share, fostering an environment where creativity can flourish. As you become more attuned to your own bodies and each other, new ideas for scenarios or fantasies are likely to arise, enhancing the overall experience and satisfaction during intimate moments.

Finally, exploring the use of toys and accessories can add a new dimension to your sexual encounters. Choose items that excite both partners, whether they be sensual massage oils, playful games, or more adventurous toys. Discussing how these accessories can be integrated into your intimate life encourages open communication and shared exploration. This not only builds trust but also enhances anticipation and pleasure. By embracing creativity in all its forms, couples can maintain sexual excitement and deepen their emotional connection, ultimately leading to a more fulfilling and satisfying sexual relationship.

5

The Role of Emotional Connection

Building Trust and Vulnerability

Building trust and vulnerability is fundamental to fostering a deeper emotional connection between partners, which can significantly enhance sexual satisfaction. When couples prioritize open communication, they create an environment where both partners feel safe to express their desires, fears, and fantasies. This transparency allows for a more profound understanding of each other's needs and enhances the overall intimacy in the relationship. Trust serves as the bedrock upon which couples can explore their sexual desires without fear of judgment, enabling them to share their most intimate thoughts and feelings.

In relationships, vulnerability often feels daunting, yet it is a crucial component in building trust. By allowing oneself to be vulnerable, partners can break down emotional barriers that may hinder their connection. This process involves taking the time to listen actively and respond empathetically to each other's feelings. Sharing personal stories, discussing past experiences, and revealing insecurities can deepen the emotional bond, paving the way for a more fulfilling sexual relationship. When both partners feel valued and understood, they are more likely to explore their sexuality together, leading to shared adventures and greater pleasure.

For couples looking to enhance their sexual experiences, incorporating vulnerability into their communication can open doors to exploring fantasies and role play. Discussing what excites each partner can lead to exciting new experiences that fulfill both emotional and physical needs. This exploration not only strengthens the bond between partners but also builds anticipation, which is crucial for maintaining sexual excitement over time. When partners feel free to express their fantasies, they can create a safe space where both can engage in role play, further igniting passion and desire.

Building anticipation through shared experiences is also essential for maintaining excitement in long-term relationships. Couples can foster this anticipation by planning intimate encounters, surprising each other with thoughtful gestures, or even indulging in playful teasing. Such actions reinforce trust and vulnerability, as they demonstrate a commitment to each other's pleasure and satisfaction. The art of foreplay becomes more than just a precursor to sex; it evolves into a vital part of the overall sexual experience that nurtures emotional connection and heightens sexual pleasure.

Mindfulness practices can further enhance the experience of building trust and vulnerability in intimate relationships. Being present with one another during intimate moments allows partners to connect deeply and appreciate the nuances of their sexual experiences. Mindfulness encourages couples to focus on the sensations, emotions, and energy exchanged between them, fostering a sense of closeness that enhances their sexual satisfaction. As couples embrace these practices, they discover that building trust and vulnerability is not just beneficial for their sexual lives but is also a pathway to a more profound, loving relationship overall.

The Impact of Emotional Intimacy on Sex

Emotional intimacy serves as the foundation for a fulfilling sexual relationship, influencing not only the desire for sex but also the quality of the sexual experience itself. When partners feel emotionally connected, they are more likely to communicate openly about their desires, preferences, and boundaries. This level of communication fosters trust, allowing each partner to express their needs without fear of judgment. As couples cultivate this emotional bond, they create a safe space where vulnerability can thrive, leading to a more satisfying sexual experience.

The interplay between emotional intimacy and sexual satisfaction is profound. Couples who prioritize their emotional connection often discover that their sexual encounters become more passionate and fulfilling. When partners share their feelings and experiences, they deepen their understanding of each other, which can enhance sexual chemistry. This emotional closeness can also lead to increased arousal, as partners feel more in tune with one another's bodies and desires. The result is a more dynamic and exciting sexual life that reflects the depth of their emotional bond.

To maintain and nurture emotional intimacy, couples should engage in regular, meaningful conversations beyond the bedroom. Discussing dreams, fears, and even fantasies can strengthen the emotional connection, making sexual encounters more vibrant. Active listening techniques, such as reflecting back what one partner has said or asking open-ended questions, can facilitate deeper discussions. These practices not only enhance communication but also promote empathy, allowing partners to feel more understood and valued, which naturally translates into a more fulfilling sexual relationship.

Incorporating elements of play and exploration into the relationship can also reinforce emotional intimacy, particularly when it comes to sexual experiences. Role play, for instance, can provide a fun and creative way for couples to express their fantasies while reinforcing their emotional bond. By stepping into different characters, partners can explore aspects of their sexuality that they might not feel comfortable discussing directly. This exploration, rooted in trust and emotional safety, can lead to exciting revelations and deeper connections during intimate moments.

Ultimately, the impact of emotional intimacy on sex is a dynamic and ongoing process. Couples who actively cultivate this intimacy through communication, exploration, and shared experiences will likely find that their sexual lives become richer and more fulfilling over time. By prioritizing emotional connection, partners set the stage for a vibrant sexual relationship that is both satisfying and sustainable, allowing them to navigate the complexities of intimacy with confidence and joy.

Strengthening the Bond

Strengthening the bond between partners is essential for cultivating a fulfilling sexual relationship. This involves more than mere physical intimacy; it requires a deep emotional connection that fosters trust, safety, and open communication. Couples can enhance their bond by prioritizing quality time together, engaging in meaningful conversations, and creating shared experiences. By being present with one another and actively listening, partners can develop a profound understanding of each other's desires, fears, and fantasies, which lays the groundwork for a more satisfying sexual connection.

One effective way to strengthen the emotional bond is through regular check-ins, where partners can openly discuss their feelings and needs. These conversations should be approached with curiosity and empathy, allowing each person to express themselves without fear of judgment. This practice not only deepens emotional intimacy but also clarifies expectations and desires related to physical intimacy. When partners feel heard and validated, they are more likely to engage in sexual activities with enthusiasm and a sense of security, knowing that their emotional needs are being met.

Exploring fantasies and role play can be another powerful method for enhancing intimacy and reigniting passion. When couples approach these topics with an open mind, they can discover new layers of attraction and excitement in their relationship. Initiating discussions about fantasies can feel vulnerable, but it also creates an opportunity for partners to understand each other on a deeper level. This exploration fosters trust and encourages a playful atmosphere, allowing couples to step outside their comfort zones and experiment with new experiences that can bring them closer together.

Building anticipation through foreplay is another crucial element in strengthening the bond between partners. Foreplay should not be seen merely as a means to an end but as an integral part of the sexual experience that enhances connection and pleasure. Couples can cultivate anticipation by incorporating various forms of touch, teasing, and playful banter into their interactions. By taking the time to explore each other's bodies and desires, partners can create a heightened sense of intimacy that not only enhances sexual satisfaction but also reinforces their emotional connection.

Finally, incorporating mindfulness practices can significantly enhance the sexual experience and strengthen the bond between partners. Being fully present during intimate moments allows couples to appreciate the nuances of their connection, from physical sensations to emotional responses. Mindfulness can help partners remain attuned to each other's needs, encouraging a deeper level of engagement and satisfaction. By embracing these practices, couples can cultivate a lasting emotional connection that not only enriches their sexual experiences but also promotes a healthy, fulfilling relationship over time.

6

The Art of Foreplay

Understanding the Importance of Foreplay

Foreplay is an essential component of a fulfilling sexual experience, serving as a bridge to deeper intimacy and connection between partners. It goes beyond mere physicality, tapping into the emotional and psychological realms that enhance sexual satisfaction. Understanding the significance of foreplay can transform your intimate encounters, turning them into moments of anticipation and excitement. By recognizing that foreplay is not simply a precursor to sex but an integral part of the experience, couples can engage more fully with each other, fostering a deeper bond.

To initiate effective foreplay, communication is key. Couples should openly discuss their desires, preferences, and boundaries, creating an environment of trust and safety. This dialogue can include what each partner enjoys, their fantasies, and any techniques that have worked well in the past. By establishing this foundation, partners can feel more confident and willing to explore each other's bodies, leading to a more enriching experience. Engaging in this conversation not only enhances the physical aspect of foreplay but also strengthens emotional intimacy, setting the stage for incredible sex.

Building anticipation is an art that can significantly enhance the foreplay experience. Taking the time to tease, touch, and verbally express attraction can heighten arousal and create a sense of eagerness. Simple gestures, such as lingering kisses, gentle caresses, or playful teasing, can make a profound difference in how partners connect. Incorporating elements of surprise or spontaneity can also keep the excitement alive, ensuring that foreplay remains a thrilling and enjoyable part of the sexual experience. This anticipation can elevate the overall connection, allowing partners to feel more in tune with one another.

Exploring fantasies and role play can add a layer of excitement to foreplay, encouraging couples to step outside their comfort zones in a safe and consensual environment. By discussing and incorporating these elements, partners can expand their sexual repertoire, discovering new ways to please each other. This exploration can be particularly valuable in long-term relationships, where routine can sometimes dampen enthusiasm. Allowing creativity to flourish within the context of foreplay can lead to a deeper understanding of each other's desires and needs, enhancing overall sexual satisfaction.

Lastly, integrating mindfulness practices into the foreplay experience can significantly enhance pleasure. Being present in the moment allows couples to fully appreciate each touch, kiss, and whisper, heightening sensations and fostering a deeper connection. Mindfulness encourages partners to focus on each other's bodies and reactions, cultivating a greater awareness of what feels good. By approaching foreplay with intention and presence, couples can transform routine encounters into extraordinary experiences that not only ignite the flame of passion but also nurture their emotional bond.

Techniques to Build Anticipation

Building anticipation in a relationship is a powerful technique that can enhance sexual experiences and deepen intimacy between partners. One effective method is through the art of teasing. This can be as simple as sending flirty texts throughout the day, hinting at what's to come later. The key is to create a sense of longing and excitement that builds as the hours pass. This playful exchange not only keeps the spark alive but also reinforces emotional connectivity, making both partners feel desired and engaged.

Another technique involves the use of sensory experiences to heighten anticipation. Engaging the senses creates a more immersive experience. Consider setting the mood with dim lighting, soft music, or even cooking a special meal together.

Incorporating scents can also be powerful; try using essential oils or scented candles that evoke a sense of intimacy. By appealing to the senses, couples can foster an environment that is ripe for connection, allowing anticipation to flourish naturally.

Communication is crucial in building anticipation. Instead of simply jumping into physical intimacy, take the time to express desires and fantasies openly. Share what excites you or ask your partner about their preferences. This dialogue not only cultivates intimacy but also allows both partners to feel more comfortable exploring their desires. When partners understand what turns each other on, they can create a roadmap that leads to thrilling experiences, making the journey just as enjoyable as the destination.

Incorporating elements of surprise can also significantly enhance anticipation. Plan unexpected date nights or surprise each other with small gifts that relate to your shared fantasies. This element of spontaneity can create a thrilling atmosphere where both partners feel invigorated by the unknown. By breaking away from routine, couples can reignite their passion and keep the flame of excitement alive, ensuring that each encounter feels fresh and invigorating.

Lastly, mindfulness practices can be a transformative way to build anticipation. By being fully present during intimate moments, partners can heighten their awareness of each other's needs and desires. Mindfulness encourages couples to focus on the sensations and emotions that arise during intimate interactions, allowing them to savor each moment. This practice not only enhances the overall sexual experience but also cultivates a deeper emotional connection, making anticipation an integral part of the journey toward incredible intimacy.

Exploring Each Other's Bodies

Exploring each other's bodies is a vital component of nurturing intimacy and enhancing sexual satisfaction in a relationship. This act goes beyond the physical; it is an invitation to connect on deeper emotional and psychological levels. To begin, it is essential for both partners to approach this exploration with an open mind and a willingness to communicate desires and boundaries. Establishing a safe space where both individuals feel comfortable expressing their needs will set the stage for a more fulfilling experience. This mutual understanding can pave the way for deeper emotional connections while also fostering an environment where vulnerability is embraced rather than feared.

As couples embark on this journey of exploration, they should focus on the art of communication. Discussing what each partner enjoys and what sensations evoke pleasure can transform the experience into a delightful dialogue rather than a one-sided encounter. This communication can take various forms—verbal affirmations, gentle touches, or even playful teasing. By actively engaging in this exchange, couples can learn more about each other's preferences, leading to a more satisfying sexual experience. This process is not only about physical touch but also about understanding emotional responses, which can significantly enhance the level of intimacy shared.

Building anticipation is crucial when exploring each other's bodies. Foreplay should be viewed as an essential part of the sexual experience, not merely a precursor to intercourse. Taking time to savor each other's skin, caress sensitive areas, and engage in prolonged moments of intimacy can heighten arousal and deepen emotional connections. Couples can use this time to experiment with different types of touch, varying pressure, and rhythms, all while ensuring that they maintain open lines of communication. This shared exploration allows partners to develop a more nuanced understanding of what excites them, ultimately contributing to a more profound connection.

Incorporating toys and accessories into this exploration can further enhance pleasure and excitement. Couples can experiment with different tools designed to stimulate various erogenous zones, adding a layer of novelty to their experiences. Discussing the use of these items openly can help demystify their role and encourage a playful attitude towards sexual exploration. This can also spark conversations about fantasies or preferences that may not have been addressed previously, thereby enriching the overall sexual experience. Additionally, the introduction of new elements can serve as a reminder that pleasure is a shared journey, encouraging partners to work together in discovering new dimensions of satisfaction.

Lastly, maintaining a sense of mindfulness during these intimate explorations is vital. Being present in the moment allows couples to fully engage with each other's sensations and emotional cues. Practicing mindfulness can enhance sexual experiences by encouraging both partners to focus on the pleasure they give and receive, rather than being distracted by external factors. This heightened awareness can lead to a more profound sense of connection and satisfaction, making each encounter a unique opportunity for growth and discovery. By fostering an environment of exploration, communication, and mindfulness, couples can ignite a flame that enhances not only their sexual experiences but also their overall relationship.

7

Incorporating Toys and Accessories

Choosing the Right Toys for Couples

Choosing the right toys for couples can significantly enhance intimacy and sexual satisfaction. The process begins with open communication about desires, boundaries, and preferences. Discussing what each partner is curious about or interested in exploring fosters a sense of connection and trust. This dialogue lays the groundwork for selecting toys that excite both partners, ensuring that the experience is enjoyable and consensual. It's essential to approach this topic with an open mind and a willingness to explore each other's fantasies, which can strengthen the emotional bond between partners.

When selecting toys, consider the variety available and how each can serve your unique relationship dynamics. Couples should explore options that cater to different interests, such as vibrators, couples' rings, or role-play accessories. Each toy offers distinct sensations and experiences that can enhance sexual pleasure and intimacy. Researching together can lead to discovering new interests and preferences, allowing you to curate a collection that reflects your shared desires and enhances your sexual journey.

Safety and comfort should remain a priority in your choices. Make sure to choose body-safe materials, such as silicone or glass, and always read product reviews to understand others' experiences. Additionally, discuss any concerns about using specific toys, ensuring that both partners feel comfortable and excited about the choices made. Setting boundaries around what is acceptable can prevent misunderstandings and create a more enjoyable experience for both partners, reinforcing the importance of consent in every aspect of your intimate life.

Incorporating toys into your sexual routine can also be a playful way to build anticipation and excitement. Consider introducing them during foreplay or as part of a romantic date night. This approach not only enhances physical pleasure but also increases emotional connection, as both partners engage in a shared experience that strengthens intimacy. By making the selection process a fun and collaborative effort, you'll encourage a sense of adventure and exploration that can invigorate your sex life.

Finally, regularly revisiting your toy collection and discussing new ideas can keep the excitement alive in a long-term relationship. As preferences evolve, so too will the types of toys that appeal to you both. Taking the time to reassess what works for you and what doesn't ensures that your sexual experiences remain fresh and fulfilling. Emphasizing ongoing communication about your desires and boundaries will strengthen your emotional connection, leading to even greater sexual satisfaction and intimacy in your relationship.

Introducing Accessories in a Fun Way

Introducing accessories into your intimate life can be a thrilling adventure that ignites passion and enhances your connection as a couple. When approached playfully, accessories can transform the ordinary into something extraordinary, creating an atmosphere rich with anticipation and excitement. Whether you're considering toys, sensual items, or even costumes, the key is to foster an environment where both partners feel comfortable and eager to explore. This chapter will guide you on how to introduce these elements in a way that enriches your relationship and deepens your emotional bond.

Start by initiating an open conversation about desires and fantasies. Set aside some time where both of you can express what excites you without judgment. This dialogue can serve as a springboard to introduce accessories that align with your shared interests. Consider using playful language and a light-hearted tone to keep the atmosphere relaxed. You might ask questions like, "Have you ever thought about trying something new in the bedroom?" or "What do you think about adding a little flair with some accessories?" This way, you create an inviting space for exploration that encourages both partners to share their thoughts and feelings.

Once you've established a comfortable dialogue, it's time to bring in the fun! You could surprise your partner with a small gift, such as a playful accessory or a toy, and present it with a sense of excitement. The element of surprise can elevate the experience, making it feel like a shared secret. Alternatively, plan a themed date night that incorporates the accessories you wish to explore. For example, if you're considering role play, you can set the scene with costumes and props that enhance the experience. The key is to keep the tone playful and enjoyable, allowing both of you to embrace the novelty.

As you begin to incorporate these accessories, remember to focus on communication and consent. Check in with each other regularly to gauge comfort levels and preferences. This ongoing dialogue not only ensures that both partners feel safe and respected but also enhances the emotional connection that is vital for sexual satisfaction. Discussing what feels good, what's exciting, and even what might be off-limits creates a foundation of trust that can lead to even greater intimacy and pleasure.

Finally, allow yourself to be spontaneous and have fun with the process. The introduction of accessories should never feel like a chore but rather an invitation to explore uncharted territories together. Keep the energy light and playful, and don't be afraid to laugh off any awkward moments. These experiences can strengthen your bond and keep the spark alive in your relationship. Embracing accessories as a part of your intimate life can lead to unforgettable moments, heightened pleasure, and a deeper emotional connection, all of which are essential for maintaining incredible sex and intimacy in your relationship.

Enhancing Pleasure Through Exploration

Enhancing pleasure through exploration is a journey that couples can embark on together, allowing them to deepen their connection and elevate their sexual experiences. It begins with an open dialogue about desires, fantasies, and boundaries. By creating a safe space for honest communication, partners can express their interests without fear of judgment. This exchange not only fosters emotional intimacy but also lays the groundwork for exploring new dimensions of pleasure, making the experience more fulfilling for both.

One effective way to enhance pleasure is by exploring fantasies and role play. Couples can discuss their fantasies, whether they involve specific scenarios, characters, or settings, to understand each other's desires better. Engaging in role play can break the monotony of routine, introducing excitement and novelty into the relationship. As partners step into different roles, they can experience heightened arousal and satisfaction, as well as gain insights into each other's preferences and boundaries.

Building anticipation through foreplay is another essential aspect of enhancing pleasure. Taking time to engage in intimate touches, kisses, and whispered words can significantly heighten sexual excitement. Couples should view foreplay as an art form, where they can creatively explore each other's bodies and build tension. This not only enhances physical pleasure but also strengthens emotional bonds, as partners become attuned to each other's needs and responses. By prioritizing foreplay, couples can transform their sexual encounters into deeply satisfying experiences.

Incorporating toys and accessories can also play a pivotal role in enhancing sexual pleasure. Couples should feel empowered to explore various tools designed to stimulate and excite. Whether it's vibrators, massage oils, or blindfolds, these additions can introduce new sensations and experiences. However, successful integration of toys requires open communication about comfort levels and preferences. By approaching the use of accessories as a shared adventure, couples can discover what truly enhances their pleasure and satisfaction.

Lastly, practicing mindfulness can significantly elevate sexual experiences. Being present in the moment allows partners to fully engage with each other, heightening physical sensations and emotional connections. Mindfulness practices can include breathing exercises, focused attention on each other's bodies, and expressing gratitude for the shared experience. By cultivating a mindful approach to intimacy, couples can foster deeper connections, ensuring that their sexual encounters are not only pleasurable but also enriching and fulfilling as they navigate their shared journey of exploration together.

8

Maintaining Sexual Excitement

Recognizing the Challenges in Long-Term Relationships

Recognizing the challenges in long-term relationships is an essential step toward fostering deeper intimacy and enhancing sexual satisfaction. As couples navigate the journey of shared life experiences, they often encounter various obstacles that can hinder their connection and diminish their sexual excitement. Acknowledging these challenges is not a sign of failure but rather an opportunity for growth and understanding. By identifying these issues, couples can work together to develop strategies that enhance communication, emotional connection, and ultimately, their sexual experiences.

One common challenge in long-term relationships is the gradual decline in sexual excitement. Over time, routines can become predictable, leading to a sense of monotony. This stagnation may cause partners to feel disconnected or even question their chemistry. To counteract this, couples can consciously shift their focus towards maintaining novelty in their intimate lives. Exploring new fantasies, incorporating toys, or experimenting with role play can reignite that initial spark. By embracing change and creativity, couples can transform their sexual encounters into dynamic and thrilling experiences.

Communication plays a crucial role in addressing the challenges that arise in a long-term partnership. Many couples struggle with openly discussing their desires and needs, which can lead to misunderstandings and resentment. Cultivating an environment where both partners feel safe to express their thoughts is fundamental. Employing effective communication techniques, such as active listening and using "I" statements, can facilitate more meaningful conversations. These discussions pave the way for deeper emotional connections, allowing partners to understand each other better and respond to each other's needs, thus enhancing their sexual relationship.

Emotional connection is another vital aspect that couples must prioritize to navigate challenges successfully. As relationships mature, emotional intimacy can either deepen or wane, impacting sexual satisfaction. Couples should invest time in nurturing their emotional bond through shared activities, quality conversations, and mindfulness practices. Engaging in these practices can help partners reconnect on a deeper level, increasing their overall satisfaction and fostering a stronger desire for one another. By prioritizing emotional intimacy, couples can create a solid foundation that supports their sexual relationship.

Lastly, maintaining sexual excitement in long-term relationships requires ongoing effort and intentionality. Couples should regularly assess their relationship dynamics, openly discussing what works and what doesn't. Building anticipation through foreplay, planning surprise dates, or setting aside dedicated time for intimacy are all effective strategies to keep the flame alive. By recognizing and addressing the challenges they face, couples can actively work towards enhancing their sexual experiences, ultimately leading to a more fulfilling and passionate connection. Acknowledging these challenges not only strengthens the partnership but also deepens the bond that fuels incredible sex.

Strategies to Keep the Spark Alive

In long-term relationships, maintaining the spark of intimacy requires intentional effort and creativity. One effective strategy is to prioritize open and honest communication about desires and fantasies. Couples should create a safe space where they can express their needs without fear of judgment. This can deepen emotional connection and lead to a better understanding of each partner's sexual preferences. Engaging in regular discussions about what excites each partner can help illuminate new paths for exploration, allowing couples to navigate their sexual landscape together with enthusiasm.

Another vital approach is to incorporate spontaneity into the relationship. Routine can dampen excitement, so finding ways to break out of the ordinary can reignite passion. This could involve surprise date nights, unexpected gestures of affection, or even spontaneous sexual encounters. Setting aside specific times for intimacy, while also leaving room for unplanned moments, can create an atmosphere of anticipation. Embracing the unexpected can lead to thrilling experiences that enhance both physical and emotional intimacy.

Exploring fantasies and role play is another dynamic way to keep the spark alive. Couples can take turns sharing their fantasies, creating a sense of adventure and discovery. Role play allows partners to step outside their usual personas, engaging in playful scenarios that can add excitement and novelty to their sexual encounters. This practice not only nurtures creativity but also fosters communication, as it requires partners to articulate their desires and boundaries clearly. By embracing these playful elements, couples can deepen their connection and enhance their sexual experiences.

Building anticipation through the art of foreplay is equally important in sustaining sexual excitement. Foreplay should not be seen merely as a prelude to intercourse; instead, it can be a way to build emotional and physical connection. Couples can experiment with different forms of touch, long kisses, and intimate conversations that heighten arousal. By taking the time to savor these moments, partners can cultivate a more profound intimacy that makes the eventual sexual encounter even more fulfilling.

Lastly, incorporating toys and accessories into the relationship can serve as an exciting way to enhance pleasure and intimacy. Couples should feel encouraged to explore new avenues of sensation together, discussing and selecting toys that appeal to both partners. This shared exploration can lead to greater understanding and satisfaction, as well as a willingness to experiment with various methods of pleasure. By being open to adding new elements to their sexual repertoire, couples can transform their experiences and keep the flame of desire burning brightly over time.

The Importance of Regular Check-Ins

In any intimate relationship, effective communication serves as the backbone that supports and nurtures the sexual connection between partners. Regular check-ins are essential for couples to discuss their desires, boundaries, and preferences, fostering an environment of openness and trust. These conversations not only help partners stay attuned to each other's needs but also create a safe space for exploring fantasies and role play. By establishing a routine for these discussions, couples can ensure that they maintain a vibrant and fulfilling sexual relationship, even as their desires evolve over time.

Regular check-ins allow partners to celebrate what is working well in their sexual lives while addressing any areas that may need attention. These moments of reflection can help couples identify patterns or habits that may be hindering their sexual excitement. Whether it is discussing the frequency of sexual encounters or pinpointing specific activities that bring pleasure, these dialogues can lead to a deeper understanding of one another. Moreover, acknowledging each other's contributions to the relationship can enhance the emotional connection, which is vital for sustaining sexual satisfaction.

Incorporating mindfulness practices during these check-ins can further enrich the experience. By being present and fully engaged in the conversation, couples can cultivate a deeper appreciation for each other's feelings and perspectives. This mindfulness fosters empathy and strengthens emotional bonds, making it easier to navigate sensitive topics such as incorporating toys and accessories or experimenting with new forms of foreplay. The more attuned partners are to each other's emotional states, the more likely they are to create a supportive atmosphere that encourages experimentation and exploration.

Anticipation is a key element in maintaining sexual excitement, and regular check-ins play a critical role in building this anticipation. During these discussions, couples can share their fantasies and desires, setting the stage for future encounters that feel fresh and exhilarating. By communicating openly about what each partner is looking forward to, couples can build excitement that extends beyond the bedroom, enriching their overall relationship. This proactive approach to intimacy helps to ensure that both partners remain engaged and invested in each other's pleasure.

Ultimately, regular check-ins are not merely a tool for problem-solving; they are a vital practice for cultivating a thriving sexual relationship. By committing to these conversations, couples can enhance their communication skills, deepen their emotional connection, and ensure that their sexual experiences remain exciting and fulfilling. Embracing the importance of these discussions allows partners to navigate the complexities of intimacy with confidence, ensuring that their sexual relationship continues to ignite passion and connection for years to come.

9

Mindfulness in the Bedroom

Practicing Presence and Awareness

Practicing presence and awareness is a vital cornerstone in enhancing sexual intimacy and satisfaction within relationships. For couples, the journey toward incredible sex begins with being fully attuned to each other, both emotionally and physically. This means engaging in mindful practices that heighten your awareness of the moment, which can lead to deeper emotional connections and more fulfilling sexual experiences. By cultivating a sense of presence, partners can better attune to each other's needs, desires, and boundaries, creating an environment where both feel safe and excited to explore their sexual relationship.

To initiate this practice, couples can start by setting aside dedicated time for each other without distractions. This could mean turning off phones, dimming the lights, or creating a serene environment that promotes relaxation. Engaging in simple mindfulness exercises, such as deep breathing or gentle touch, can help both partners center themselves and become attuned to their own bodies. This practice not only fosters an atmosphere of comfort but also encourages open communication about desires and boundaries. When both partners are present, they can better express what feels good, leading to a more satisfying sexual experience.

In addition to creating a distraction-free environment, couples can enhance their presence by engaging in activities that promote intimacy outside of the bedroom. This might include shared hobbies, regular date nights, or simply taking walks together. These moments allow partners to connect emotionally, reinforcing their bond and making sexual encounters more meaningful. When couples prioritize emotional connection, they are more likely to feel comfortable exploring fantasies and role play, further enhancing their sexual experiences. The emotional foundation built during these shared activities can be a catalyst for increased sexual excitement and exploration.

Incorporating mindfulness into foreplay is another effective way to maintain sexual excitement in long-term relationships. Rather than rushing through the experience, partners can savor each moment, focusing on the sensations of touch, taste, and sound. This slow and deliberate approach not only heightens arousal but also builds anticipation for what's to come. By practicing presence in these intimate moments, couples can discover new levels of pleasure and intimacy, ensuring that their sexual relationship remains vibrant and fulfilling over time.

Finally, couples should remember that practicing presence and awareness is an ongoing journey. It requires patience, commitment, and a willingness to explore new avenues of intimacy together. As partners continue to refine their communication techniques and deepen their emotional connection, they will find that their sexual experiences become richer and more satisfying. By embracing mindfulness as a core component of their relationship, couples can ignite the flame of incredible sex, transforming their intimate lives into a dynamic and fulfilling adventure.

Techniques for Mindful Touch

Mindful touch is a powerful tool for couples seeking to deepen their intimacy and enhance their sexual experiences. It begins with the fundamental principle of being fully present in the moment, focusing on the sensations and emotions that arise during physical connection. To practice mindful touch, set aside distractions and create a space that feels safe and inviting. This could involve dimming the lights, playing soft music, or even using aromatherapy to stimulate the senses. As you engage in touch, pay attention to the ways your partner responds, both physically and emotionally, allowing this awareness to guide your actions.

One effective technique is to establish a gentle, exploratory touch that prioritizes connection over performance. Instead of rushing into more stimulating or familiar movements, take time to explore each other's bodies with deliberate slowness. Use your fingertips to trace contours, experiment with different pressures, and vary your rhythm. This not only fosters a deeper emotional bond but also builds anticipation. As you both become more attuned to each other's responses, you'll discover new erogenous zones and preferences, enhancing your overall sexual satisfaction.

Incorporating breathing exercises can further amplify the experience of mindful touch. Synchronizing your breath with your partner's can create a rhythm that enhances intimacy. As you touch, inhale deeply and exhale slowly, allowing the breath to flow through both of you. This practice encourages relaxation and presence, making it easier to connect on a deeper level. Additionally, consider voicing what you feel or what you enjoy during this process. Open communication about sensations and desires fosters trust and encourages exploration, allowing for a more fulfilling sexual experience.

Fantasy and role play can also play a significant role in mindful touch. Engaging in scenarios that excite both partners can help cultivate an atmosphere of playfulness and discovery. Discussing fantasies openly can lead to deeper emotional connections and increased sexual satisfaction. Once a fantasy is chosen, incorporate mindful touch that aligns with the scenario. This not only enhances the experience but also strengthens the bond between partners as they explore new dynamics together. The key is to remain present and engaged, allowing the experience to unfold naturally.

Finally, integrating the use of toys and accessories can elevate the art of mindful touch. Selecting items that both partners feel comfortable with adds an element of novelty and excitement to the experience. As you incorporate these tools, maintain the principles of mindfulness by focusing on how each new sensation affects both partners. Be open to feedback, adjusting your approach based on each other's reactions. This practice not only enhances pleasure but also nurtures a deeper emotional connection, making each encounter more memorable. Through mindful touch, couples can ignite the flame of intimacy, transforming their sexual experiences into profound expressions of love and connection.

Enhancing Connection Through Mindfulness

Enhancing connection through mindfulness is a powerful approach that couples can use to deepen their intimacy and elevate their sexual experiences. Mindfulness involves being fully present in the moment, allowing partners to engage with each other on a deeper emotional and physical level. By practicing mindfulness, couples can cultivate a heightened awareness of their own bodies, desires, and sensations, as well as those of their partners. This practice not only fosters better communication but also creates a safe space for exploring fantasies and desires that might otherwise go unexpressed.

To begin incorporating mindfulness into your relationship, set aside dedicated time for connection without distractions. This could mean turning off electronic devices, creating a comfortable environment, or even engaging in a shared activity like meditation or yoga. During these moments, focus on each other's breath, touch, and energy. Gentle touches and eye contact can enhance this experience, allowing both partners to feel more attuned to one another. This awareness lays the groundwork for emotional connection, which is essential for sexual satisfaction and can significantly enhance your overall relationship.

As you grow more accustomed to mindfulness practices, consider integrating them into your sexual encounters. Start by savoring the sensations of touch, kiss, or even the anticipation that builds before intimacy. Encourage your partner to express what feels good, and practice active listening to understand their needs better. This moment-to-moment awareness can transform the sexual experience into something much richer and more fulfilling, where both partners feel seen and appreciated. Embracing this level of presence can also make it easier to introduce new elements, such as toys or role play, since the foundation of trust and communication is already established.

In addition to enhancing the physical aspects of intimacy, mindfulness can play a crucial role in maintaining sexual excitement in long-term relationships. By continually checking in with each other's desires and boundaries, couples can keep the flame alive. Regular mindfulness practices can help individuals recognize when they start to drift apart emotionally or physically, allowing them to address issues before they escalate. This proactive approach fosters a deeper emotional connection, ensuring that both partners feel valued and understood, which is vital for sustaining a satisfying sexual relationship.

Ultimately, enhancing connection through mindfulness is about creating a shared journey of discovery and intimacy. As couples practice being present with one another, they cultivate a safe and loving environment where both partners can explore their desires freely. This commitment to mindfulness not only enriches sexual experiences but also strengthens the emotional bond that forms the bedrock of any successful relationship. By prioritizing this connection, couples can ignite a passion that endures, ensuring that their sexual lives remain vibrant and fulfilling for years to come.

10

Creating a Personalized Communication Plan

Setting Goals for Sexual Communication

Setting goals for sexual communication is an essential step for couples looking to enhance their intimate lives. By establishing clear objectives, partners can create a shared understanding of their desires, boundaries, and expectations. This process begins with open dialogue where both individuals express their needs and aspirations without fear of judgment. By treating these discussions as a collaborative effort, couples can foster a safe space that encourages vulnerability and honesty, laying the groundwork for deeper emotional and physical connections.

One effective way to approach goal-setting is to identify specific areas of sexual communication that each partner wishes to improve. This could include initiating conversations about fantasies, discussing preferences for foreplay, or exploring the incorporation of toys and accessories. By pinpointing these areas, couples can prioritize aspects of their sexual relationship that may have been neglected or overlooked. Setting measurable and achievable goals, such as scheduling regular check-ins about each other's desires, can help maintain focus and progress.

In addition to identifying improvement areas, couples should also set goals that promote emotional connection. Understanding each partner's emotional needs is crucial for sexual satisfaction. Couples can aim to enhance their emotional intimacy by engaging in activities that promote bonding outside the bedroom, such as date nights or shared hobbies. These experiences can serve as a foundation for more profound sexual discussions, reinforcing the idea that emotional connection is integral to physical pleasure.

Maintaining excitement in long-term relationships requires ongoing communication and adaptability. Couples should set goals that encourage exploration and spontaneity, such as trying new activities together or discussing new fantasies. This approach not only keeps the sexual relationship vibrant but also strengthens the overall bond between partners. Establishing a "bucket list" of experiences to explore can ignite anticipation and enthusiasm, creating opportunities for shared adventures that go beyond the routine.

Finally, incorporating mindfulness practices can significantly enhance sexual experiences and communication. Setting goals related to mindfulness can help partners become more attuned to each other's needs and desires. This could involve practicing mindfulness techniques, such as breathing exercises or guided intimacy sessions, to create a more present and connected experience during sexual encounters. By fostering awareness and presence, couples can deepen their intimacy and create a more fulfilling sexual relationship that thrives on clear communication and shared goals.

Regularly Revisiting and Adjusting the Plan

Regularly revisiting and adjusting your sexual intimacy plan is essential for maintaining a vibrant and fulfilling sexual relationship. Just as life circumstances, desires, and emotional states evolve, so too should your approach to intimacy. Taking the time to reflect on your experiences together fosters an environment where both partners feel heard and valued. This practice not only enhances communication but also deepens the emotional connection that is crucial for sexual satisfaction. By engaging in open dialogues about each other's needs, preferences, and fantasies, you can ensure both partners remain aligned and excited about their intimate life.

One effective way to approach adjustments in your intimacy plan is through regular check-ins. Set aside time, free from distractions, to discuss what has been working and what hasn't. This could be a weekly or monthly ritual where you can explore feelings, desires, and any challenges that may have arisen. Use this time not only as a platform for sharing but also for brainstorming new ideas to keep the flame alive. Whether it be trying out new techniques, exploring fantasies, or incorporating toys and accessories, these discussions can offer opportunities for growth and exploration, making your connection even stronger.

Another key aspect of revisiting your plan is the recognition of changes in individual circumstances. Stress from work, changes in health, or shifts in family dynamics can all impact your sexual relationship. Acknowledging these changes allows you to be more compassionate towards each other's needs. When one partner is feeling overwhelmed or distracted, it might be a signal to focus more on nurturing emotional connection through simple acts of affection or dedicated quality time rather than pushing for a more intense sexual experience. Flexibility and understanding become the cornerstones of a healthy sexual relationship, enabling both partners to adapt to each other's changing emotional landscapes.

Incorporating mindfulness practices can also enhance the process of revisiting your intimacy plan. Mindfulness encourages you to be present with each other, fostering a deeper understanding of your partner's desires and sensations. By being more attuned to the moment, you can identify what feels good, what excites you both, and what may need adjustment. Consider engaging in mindfulness exercises together, such as synchronized breathing or guided intimacy meditations. These practices not only deepen emotional connection but also create a safe space for exploring new ideas and desires, enriching your sexual experiences.

Finally, remember that the journey of enhancing sexual intimacy is ongoing and should be embraced with curiosity and enthusiasm. Rather than viewing adjustments as a chore, approach them as an adventure where both partners can explore new dimensions of pleasure and connection. Celebrate the discoveries you make together, whether in the bedroom or during your discussions. By regularly revisiting and adjusting your intimacy plan, you are committing to a dynamic and fulfilling sexual relationship that grows and evolves alongside both partners, igniting the flame of passion and intimacy for years to come.

Celebrating Progress Together

Celebrating progress together is an essential aspect of nurturing intimacy and enhancing sexual satisfaction in any relationship. When couples actively acknowledge and celebrate their achievements, whether big or small, they reinforce their emotional connection. This shared recognition not only deepens the bond between partners but also creates a positive environment where both individuals feel valued and understood. Celebrating progress can manifest in various forms, from verbal affirmations to small gestures that signify appreciation, and it plays a crucial role in maintaining enthusiasm and excitement in the relationship.

One way to celebrate progress is through open communication about the milestones reached in the bedroom. Couples can take time to reflect on the improvements they have made in their sexual connection, such as trying new techniques, exploring fantasies, or incorporating toys and accessories. By discussing these developments, partners can express their satisfaction and excitement, which reinforces emotional intimacy. Celebrating these achievements can transform routine moments into special occasions, fostering a sense of accomplishment that enhances overall relationship satisfaction.

In addition to verbal communication, physical celebrations can also be a powerful tool for couples. Engaging in affectionate gestures, such as a surprise date night or a romantic getaway, can serve as a tangible acknowledgment of the progress made. These moments allow couples to step away from daily routines and focus on each other, reigniting passion and enthusiasm. By creating lasting memories tied to their sexual journey, couples can reinforce their commitment to maintaining excitement and intimacy in their relationship.

Furthermore, couples can establish rituals that honor their progress. These can include regular check-ins where both partners discuss their desires, aspirations, and any areas of improvement. By creating a safe space for these conversations, couples can celebrate their victories and address challenges collaboratively. This ongoing dialogue not only strengthens the emotional connection but also reinforces the idea that both partners are invested in each other's pleasure and satisfaction, fostering a sense of teamwork in the relationship.

Ultimately, celebrating progress together is not just about acknowledging achievements; it is about cultivating a mindset of gratitude and appreciation within the relationship. By recognizing the efforts made in enhancing intimacy, couples can create a positive feedback loop that encourages further exploration and experimentation. This practice not only enhances sexual experiences but also strengthens the emotional bond, ensuring that both partners feel cherished and fulfilled in their journey together. In this way, celebrating progress becomes a vital component of an incredible sexual relationship, paving the way for ongoing growth and connection.